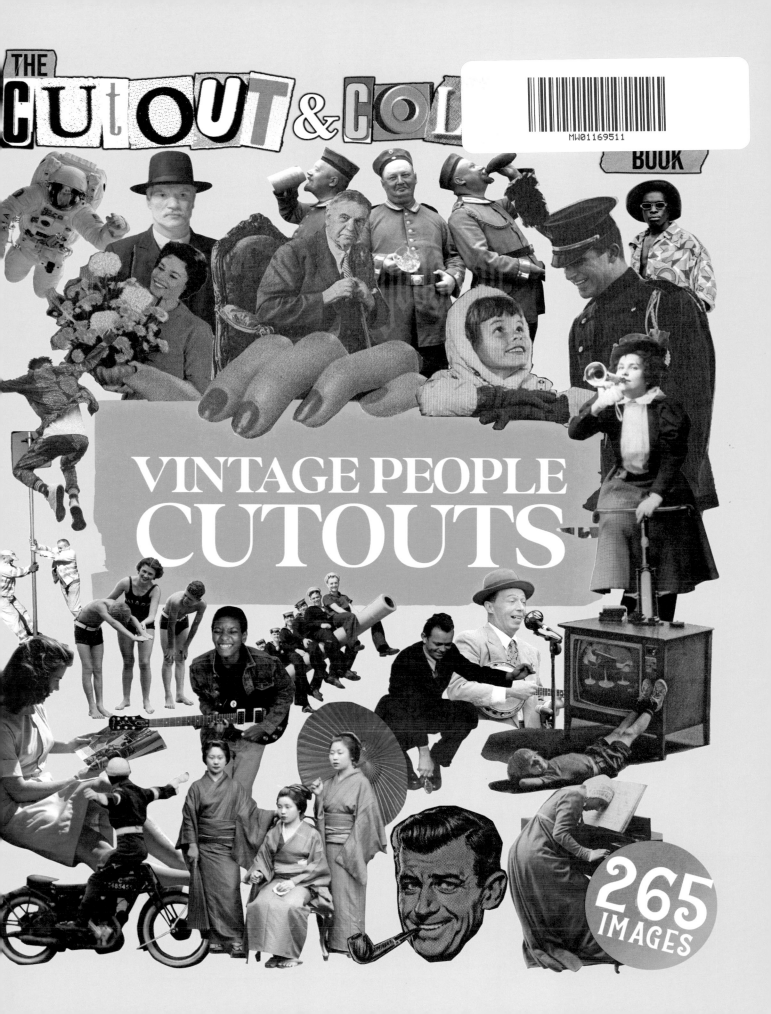

THE CUTOUT & COLOR BOOK

VINTAGE PEOPLE CUTOUTS

265 IMAGES

COLLAGE HEAVEN

WWW.COLLAGEHEAVEN.COM

COLLAGE HEAVEN IS A SMALL STUDIO RUN BY ARTISTS FOR ARTISTS.
WE CREATE SUPPLIES THAT ARE USUALLY HARD TO FIND AND TIME-CONSUMING AND PROVIDE THEM AT AFFORDABLE PRICES AND IN AN ORGANIZED WAY SO YOU, AS AN ARTIST OR HOBBYIST, CAN FOCUS ON CREATING AND LET US DO RESEARCH AND PROVIDE YOU WITH THE SUPPLIES YOU NEED FOR YOUR WORK!

WE'D LOVE TO HEAR YOUR HONEST OPINION

★★★★★

WWW.COLLAGEHEAVEN.COM

+ Follow

**Follow To Get New Release Updates
And Improved Recommendations**

SCAN ME!

NEW ORLEANS 330 MI.

DIVE
AT OWN
RISK

Made in United States
Troutdale, OR
02/15/2025

28984764R00033